O H I O   G L A S S

1815-1953

THE TOLEDO MUSEUM OF ART

October 1953

OHIO GLASS

Since the early nineteenth century,
not long after the establishment of the
territory as a State, glassmaking has
been one of the major industries of Ohio,
and Ohio glass holds an important place
in the development of the industry in the
United States.

Throughout American history we find
that the record of glassmaking follows
closely the establishment of settlements -
first in Virginia, then Pennsylvania, New
Jersey, New York and New England; later
westward to the Ohio Valley and the Great
Lakes. John Smith's History of Virginia,
published in 1632, states that glass was
made at Jamestown, but by 1625 there was
no longer a glass furnace in existence
there. For more than one hundred years
there were sporadic attempts to produce
glass in the Colonies, but not until 1739,
when Caspar Wistar founded his factory in
Salem County, New Jersey, was a glass works
established which had a continued existence
for any length of time. The glass made
here was called Wistarberg and was the
beginning of the style generally called
South Jersey. Henry William Stiegel,
known as "Baron" Stiegel, founded a glass
house at Mannheim, Pennsylvania, where he
produced fine glassware from 1769 to 1773.
He imitated the contemporary English and
Continental glass and was in turn the
leading influence upon the glass workers
who crossed the Alleghenies and founded
or worked in the factories of Western
Pennsylvania and Ohio. The first glass

house west of the Alleghenies was established by Albert Gallatin, noted
statesman and founder of New York
University.

The first quarter of the nineteenth century had seen the country
through a financial crisis. By 1820
to 1825 conditions had begun to improve.
Domestic manufacture was being encour-
aged by the government and ambitious
pioneers were building homes in Western
New York, Pennsylvania, West Virginia,
and Eastern Ohio. Many of those who
moved west had left comfortable homes
in the East, and needed tableware,
lamps, candlesticks, and other objects
of glass. By 1840 there were eight
glass factories in Ohio well established.

Until about twenty years ago almost
nothing was known about the Ohio and other
Midwestern glass houses which operated in
the nineteenth century. We owe our knowledge in great part to the researches of
Rhea Mansfield Knittle of Ashland, Ohio,
whose book, Early American Glass, was
published in 1927. She established that
the first glass house in Ohio was at
Zanesville, organized by a group of
citizens and incorporated May 13, 1815,
as the White Glass Works. An announce-
ment of 1816 stated:
  "These works are now in complete operation, and the proprietors have on hand
  a large assortment of white hollow ware,
  specimens of which may be seen at their
  warehouse. Physicians and apothecaries
  can be furnished with ware for shop
  furniture. Orders shall be filled with
  care and despatch, and upon as reason-

able terms as can be purchased in the western country."

In 1822 Joseph Shepard and others purchased the factory, using the name Shepard & Company. Much of the fine early glass now known to have been made in Ohio was probably produced there. Except for a few flasks there were no marked pieces. In 1842 a new organization, Kearns & Company, took over the works; and in 1848 built a new plant at Putnam, across the Muskingum River from Zanesville, which remained in operation for many years. Some of the later pictorial flasks were made there.

In 1816 another glass house was built in Zanesville. Under the name of the New Granite Glass Works it was operated first by James Taylor and Alexander Culbertson, until both died suddenly in 1823, then by Murdock and Cassell under that name until some time in the 1840's. A number of flasks are known to have been made there, some marked with the name. One of the rarest pieces of Ohio glass is the light green quart decanter blown in a two-piece mould with the inscription "Murdock and Cassell, Zanesville". To date only one specimen is recorded. It is illustrated in McKearin, American Glass, Pl. 81, Nos. 1 and 4.

While bottles and flasks were the principal commercial products of these glass houses, some fine tableware was also made. Plain free-blown, or pattern moulded bowls, pitchers, sugar bowls, salts, in ribbed, swirled, diamond, and other designs were made

in a wide range of colors. For many
years these pattern-moulded wares from
the Ohio area were accepted as Stiegel,
and are now often referred to as Ohio
Stiegel. It is possible that some of
the workmen who came to these Midwest
factories had been trained by Stiegel
or his workers, for after the failure
of the Stiegel factory the workmen
were widely scattered, and following
the Revolution, many of them migrated
westward.

Our knowledge of another Ohio glass
factory came through the researches of
the late Harry Hall White in the early
1930's. The story of his discoveries
published in Antiques Magazine in 1934
and 1935 is a fascinating one. At
Mantua, in Portage County, David Ladd
of Connecticut, associated with
Jonathan Tinker of Vernon, New York,
started operations in 1821, when the
settlement consisted of scarcely more
than a few log houses, a mill and a
tavern. The Mantua Glass Company completed its plant in 1822, and in the
Western Reserve Chronicle published
at Warren, Ohio, on February 9, 1822,
the following appeared:

   "We have lately received as a present
   from the proprietors of the glass
   works in Mantua, a very clear well-
   shaped decanter and elegant sweet-
   meat, as a specimen of their skill
   in the important manufacture in which
   they are engaged. Both of these
   articles are ample proof of the
   ability of the enterprising and
   meritorious owners of this establishment to serve the public in their
   line of business. We hope they will

receive all the encouragement neces-
sary for the support and prosperity
of their highly useful undertaking."

Later both Ladd and Tinker built
glass houses on the Cuyahoga River, at
Carthage and Franklin Mills, which were
so close together that they were incorporated as the town of Kent. Both had
brought with them from the East the tra-
ditions of glassmaking - perhaps even
some of the moulds used there. At both
Mantua and Kent free-blown and pattern-
moulded glass was made, and three-mould
blown as well. The three-mould patterns
are combinations of diamond and ribs in
various arrangements and are seen in
decanters, pitchers, flips and bowls.

Around the middle of the 1800's,
there were many glass factories established. At Putnam, directly across from
Zanesville, John Carter of Pennsylvania
built the Putnam Flint Glass Works, later
Carter and Woodruff, which made flint
glass hollow ware of all types. At one
time they employed 200 men, and accord-
ing to an old advertisement, put out
"milk pans with reamed edges, wide-necked
and rather straight-sided pitchers, chem-
ical apparatus, druggists supplies, pickle
and caper bottles, candlesticks, cruets,
sugar bowls, glass balls, hollow glass
dippers, globes, and many other commod-
ities." This factory became in 1881 the
home of the Haines patent fruit jar.

At Kent a later glass plant was
completed in 1851. The firm was known
as Kent, Mills and Company. Before 1864
this factory turned out a large quantity

of swirled bottles of the Zanesville type
in light green, bluish green, and amber.
After the Civil War the company made
chiefly window glass.

At Ravenna, Ohio, not far from Kent,
the Ravenna Glass Company began to operate
in 1857 and continued until 1864. It was
especially known for historical and pictorial bottles and flasks. The Ravenna
flasks are of very good quality and some
of them are marked. The Jenny Lind bottle
with one N in Jenny and a factory on the
reverse was made there.

Another part of Ohio which was active
in the field of glass early in the nineteenth century was at the eastern end of
the Ohio River. At Steubenville a glass
furnace was built in 1830 by Kilgore and
Hanna of Pittsburgh. About 1850 when
A.J. Beatty took over the business, the
factory had a flourishing trade in goblets. They made a high grade goblet which
sold cheaply and soon this factory was
producing enough to supply the whole
country. They were shipped also to every
port in the world and when production was
at its height, the company employed 160
men and the average daily output was
36,000 goblets and tumblers. The Steubenville firm became a world leader in these
products, competing successfully with
imported glass from England, France and
Germany. The glass industry was a force
in building up the town of Steubenville,
which became the home of many glass
workers. Between 1870 and 1880, endless
varieties of colored pressed tableware
were made there.

Of the factories in existence in the 1880-90 period which made quantities of pressed and blown glass in the popular styles of the day, cnly a few are still operating. They were located throughout the State from the Ohio River to Lake Erie and from Pennsylvania to Indiana. Findlay, Bowling Green, Tiffin, and Fostoria in this area were notable centers. Findlay, which had sixteen factories at one time, and Bowling Green, with five, no longer have glass manufacturing plants. At Tiffin we now find the U.S. Glass Company, an outgrowth of the factory founded in the 1880's and taken over by the great trust, which absorbed many of the smaller plants. The Fostoria Glass Company moved to Moundsville, W. Va., where they are still operating. Heisey is one of the factories dating from the 1890's, still at Newark, Ohio. The Libbey Glass Company had its start in Toledo in 1888.

Northwestern Ohio became the center of glassmaking when natural gas was discovered in this region. Economical and satisfactory as a fuel, it was partly responsible for the choice of Toledo as the factory site for the New England Glass Company, which Edward Drummond Libbey moved here from East Cambridge, Mass. The New England Glass Company, established in 1818, had made fine glassware since its beginning. During the 1880's, when the fashion of colored glass was at its height, several new types were invented, among them Amberina, Pomona, Peachblow, Burmese, etc. The most popular was Amberina, the ruby color achieved by the use of gold in the glass mixture,

and the red shading to pale amber obtained by reheating. The Libbey Glass
Company name was adopted in 1891, and
received world recognition at the
Columbian Exposition of 1893 at Chicago
where visitors saw all types of glass
being made, and examples of the fine
heavy cut glass, then the chief production of the Libbey Glass Company.

From 1890 to 1915 was the era of
cut glass, with a number of companies
making useful and decorative pieces.
Cut glass, however, was expensive and
many factories which had been making
pressed glass in simple, attractive
patterns, now turned to imitating the
elaborate designs of cut glass. These
cheaper wares, mass-produced, and the
decorated colored blown glass, commonly
called "art glass" which flooded the
market, brought about the downfall of
many factories, which had prospered
for a time.

From about 1920, with the change
in the types of homes in which people
lived, the problem of household help,
and the simplification of the style of
living, the demand for elaborate glassware waned. Simple, well-designed
tableware and decorative pieces were,
and still are, being produced by both
handblown and machine methods. In Ohio,
such factories as Cambridge, at Cambridge,
Ohio, Imperial at Bellaire, Ohio, Heisey
at Newark, Ohio, U.S. Glass at Tiffin, and
Libbey at Toledo, present fine examples
of attractive glass of high quality, con-
tinuing the century-long history of Ohio
as a glassmaking center.

CATALOGUE

ZANESVILLE GLASS

Lent by George S. McKearin,
Hoosick Falls, N. Y.

1. Sugar Bowl - light olive green,
   diamond moulded. (Cover missing)
2. Sugar Bowl - deep amber; expanded
   vertical ribbing. Dome-shaped
   cover, diamond moulded.
3. Bowl - amber. Diamond-moulded.
4. Pitcher - light moonstone, diamond
   moulded. Only specimen so far
   recorded in this color.
5. Bottle - cornflower blue. Rib moulded.
6. Inkwell - amber. Rib moulded.
7. Bowl - yellow amber. Free blown.
8. Flip glass - cornflower blue.
9. Flask - light green. Melon shape,
   vertical ribbing.
10-17. Chestnut flasks. Diamond moulded.
18. Chestnut flask - light yellow amber.
    Swirled ribbing.
19. Chestnut flask - light amber. Vertical
    ribbing. Collared lip.
20. Chestnut flask - broken swirl pattern.
21. Pitcher - deep blue, neck threaded.
22. Tumbler - brilliant green. Rib moulded.
23. Tumbler - reddish amber. Rib moulded.

Lent by J. R. Rodgers,
Slippery Rock, Pennsylvania

24. Vase - light green. Swirled ribbing.
    Two-handled.
25. Bowl - yellow green. Broken - swirl
    pattern.
26. Bowl - green. Rib moulded.

27. Flip - green. Broken swirl pattern.
28. Flip - amber. Swirled ribbing.
29. Decanter with stopper - green.
30. Salt - amethyst.
31. Chestnut flask - green. Diamond-
    quilted.
32. Chestnut flask - clear. Diamond-
    quilted.
33. Chestnut flask - golden amber.
    Diamond-quilted.
34. Chestnut flask - dark amber.
    Diamond-quilted.
35. Chestnut flask - green. Swirl
    pattern.
36. Chestnut flask - amber. Swirl
    pattern.
37. Chestnut flask - dark amber. Broken
    swirl pattern.
38. Flask - amber. Expanded vertical
    ribbing. Called Grandfather Flask.
39. Flask - aquamarine. Expanded
    vertical ribbing. Called Grand-
    mother Flask.
40. Goblet - dark amber. Footed.
41. Goblet - light green.

        Lent by The Art Institute
        of Zanesville.

42. Sugar Bowl - deep cobalt blue with
    double-domed cover.
43. Compote - olive-amber.
44. Bulb Vase - emerald green and clear.
45. Vase - deep amber with ball cover.
46. Pitcher - light green. Swirl pattern.
47. Pitcher - brilliant aquamarine.
    Diamond moulded.
48. Pitcher - large cylindrical, clear
    glass with engraved inscription
    "Jacob Kappes-Putnam Hotel". Made
    1850-60.

Lent by Earl J. Knittle
Ashland, Ohio

49-102. Collection of globular bottles,
      Zanesville type.
103. Ball - amber. Swirled pattern.
104. Bottle with handle - dark amber.

From Toledo Museum of Art Collection

105. Chestnut flask - olive green with
    brown streaks. Diamond-quilted.

MANTUA GLASS

Lent by George S. McKearin

106. Decanter - light green. Blown three-
    mould in Pattern G II-18 (McKearin).
107. Bowl - amber. Rib moulded.
108. Bowl - yellow amber. Rib moulded.
109. Salt - yellow amber. Rib moulded.
110. Tumbler - light green. Broken swirl
    pattern. Rib moulded. Originally in
    collection of Harry Hall White.
111. Salt - yellow amber. Urn-shaped.
    Rib moulded.
112. Salt cup - yellow green. Ogee shape.
    Rib moulded.
113. Toilet or vinegar bottle - olive
    yellowish-green. Swirled ribbing.
114. Bowl - amethyst of unusual trans-
    lucent shade.
115. Flask - olive yellow. Rib moulded.
116. Chestnut flask - yellow green.
    Vertical ribbing.
117. Chestnut flask - light green.
    Swirled ribbing.
118. Flask. Flattened ovoid form.
    Diamond moulded.

Lent by J. R. Rodgers

119. Bowl - amethyst, light and dark
     striations.
120. Miniature bowl - clear. Broken
     swirl pattern.
121. Miniature mug - amethyst. Broken
     swirl pattern.

Lent by Earl J. Knittle

122. Globular bottle - deep aquamarine.
     Ribbed pattern. Formerly in the
     Harry Hall White Collection.

KENT GLASS

Lent by George S. McKearin

123. Bowl - light green. Blown three-
     mould. Pattern II-6 (McKearin).
124. Decanter - yellow green. Blown
     three-mould. Pattern II-6
     (McKearin).
125. Decanter with applied neck rings.
     Clear, blown three-mould.
     Pattern II-6 (McKearin).
126. Bowl - reddish amber. Rib moulded.
127. Decanter - light green. Blown
     three-mould. Pattern II-6
     (McKearin).

Lent by J. R. Rodgers

128. Bowl with foot - olive green.
     Blown three-mould. Only one of
     this type known.

Lent by Earl J. Knittle

129. Decanter - light green. Blown
     three-mould.

130. Decanter - light jade green, semi-opaque glass. Blown three-mould.

STEUBENVILLE GLASS

Lent by George S. McKearin

131. Chalice - deep blue. (Reproduced Pl. 80, No. 13, McKearin, American Glass.)
132. Pitcher - clear glass. Free blown, silver half dime dated 1833 in large hollow knop of stem.

EARLY OHIO GLASS - MISCELLANEOUS

Lent by George S. McKearin

133. Salt cup - brilliant amethyst. Broken swirl decoration.
134. Bowl - light green. Shallow form, broken swirl decoration.
135. Bowl - amethyst. Footed; rib moulded.
136. Bowl - yellow amber. Free-blown with flaring sides, heavy folded rim.

Lent by Mrs. Paul Cropper, Mansfield, Ohio

137. Pitcher - heavy, dark amber.

PITKIN TYPE FLASKS

Lent by George S. McKearin

138. Light green, broken swirl decoration.
139. Brilliant green, broken swirl decoration.

140. Brilliant green, broken swirl
    decoration.
141. Light green, half pint, broken
    swirl decoration.
142. Yellow amber, broken swirl
    decoration.

Collection of Toledo Museum of Art

143. Green, broken swirl decoration.

All of these flasks are made in 32-rib
moulds. Parry Hall White's excavations
show that Pitkin flasks patterned in
such moulds were made at the Mantua
Glass Works.

HISTORICAL BOTTLES AND FLASKS

Lent by George S. McKearin

144. J. Shepard & Co., Zanesville.
    Pint, light green. G IV-32.
145. J. Shepard & Co., Zanesville.
    Pint, dark amber (black glass).
146. J. Shepard & Co., Zanesville.
    Pint, light olive green.
147. Zanesville. Half pint, reddish
    amber. Eagle and cornucopia.
    G II-18.
148. Zanesville. Half pint, light
    green.
149. Flask - light green pint. Marked
    "Murdock & Cassell, Zanesville,
150. Flask - aquamarine. Eagle on
    each side, rectangular frame
    with inscription "Zanesville
    Ohio" on one side.

151. Flask - olive green, pint. Prospector
     with bottle to lips; reverse, eagle
     and rectangular frame. This particular
     Pike's Peak flask is attributed to
     one of the Zanesville glass houses.
152. Flask - yellow green, pint. Oval
     frame on one side with inscription
     "Zanesville City Glass Works".
153. Flask - deep amber. Similar to 151.
154. Calabash bottle - brilliant green.
     Bust of Jenny Lind and inscription
     "JENY LIND"; reverse, view of glass
     house. Attributed to Ravenna Glass
     Works, Ravenna, Ohio. G I-105.
155. Calabash bottle - sapphire blue.
     Similar to 153.
156. Calabash bottle - aquamarine.
     Similar to 153 and 154, except smoke
     from chimney going upward instead
     of turning down.
157. Flask - yellow and olive tone, pint.
     Eagle and 13 stars; reverse, anchor
     and inscription "Ravenna Glass Com-
     pany". G II-37.
158. Flask - deep amber, pint. Large
     8-pointed star and inscription
     "Traveler's Companion"; reverse,
     "Ravenna Glass Co.".
159. Flask - deep green, quart.
     Similar design to 157.
160. Flask - aquamarine. Large 5-pointed
     star; reverse, "Ravenna Glass Works".

     Lent by J. R. Rodgers

161. Flask - aquamarine. Similar to 157.

     Collection of Toledo Museum of Art

162. Flask - dark amber. Similar to 143.

163. Calabash bottle - cornflower blue.
     Similar to 153.
164. Scroll flask - dark amber

PRESSED GLASS 1870-1900

Lent by Mr. and Mrs. Chester
Pendleton, Findlay, Ohio

165. Findlay Silver Inlay Vase.
166. Findlay Silver Inlay Syrup Jug.
167. Vase - variation of 164 in purple
     lustre.
168. Vase - variation of 164 in black.
169. Sugar Bowl and Cream Pitcher -
     variation of 164 in light ruby
     and opaque white.
170. Amberette Vase.
171. Priscilla Pattern Bowl.

All made by Dalzell, Gillmore and
Leighton Co., Findlay, Ohio. 1890-1900.

Lent by Mrs. John Dillman,
Findlay

172-77. Six pieces of pressed glass
        made by Dalzell, Gillmore &
        Leighton Co. 1890-1901.

Lent by A. H. Heisey Glass Co.,
Newark, Ohio

178-81. Pressed glass made by
        A. H. Heisey Glass Co., Newark,
        Ohio. 1895-1900.

Lent by Mr. and Mrs. Roland E.
Deitemeyer, Toledo

182-86. Hobnail with Diamond Band.
Made by the Columbia Glass Co.,
Findlay, Ohio, 1888-89.

Lent by Lucile Hughes, Toledo

187. Old Man of the Woods Pattern.
Martins Ferry, Ohio, 1879.
188. Opal Coin Dot Pattern.
Martins Ferry, Ohio, 1895.

Lent by Mrs. E. M. Belknap,
Toledo

189-91. Actress Pattern.
Bridgeport, Ohio, 1879.
192. Sugar Bowl. Frosted Eagle Pattern.
Bridgeport, Ohio, 1879
193-94. Libbey Maize Pattern, 1889.

LIBBEY GLASS 1888-1900

Collection of Toledo Museum of Art

CONTEMPORARY GLASS

Lent by

Cambridge Glass Co., Cambridge, Ohio
A. H. Heisey Glass Co., Newark, Ohio
Imperial Glass Corp., Bellaire, Ohio
Libbey Division, Owens-Illinois
  Glass Company, Toledo
United States Glass Co., Tiffin, Ohio
Collection of Toledo Museum of Art

CPSIA information can be obtained
at www.ICGtesting.com
Printed in the USA
BVHW050629070423
661944BV00020B/155